A BOOK OF PRAYERS

BY

Edwin R. Larson

"A Book of Prayers
by Edwin R. Larson

Published by:
Shuffling Papers, a division of
Edwin R. Larson, M.D., Inc.
9200 Montgomery Road, Suite 8A.

. ISBN: 9798619647563

Dedication

I am in debt to my beautiful wife, Linda, who keeps me grounded.
I am thankful for Father George Hill who truly practices what he preaches.
I am grateful for Trevor, Max, and Dane who teach me about growth.
I am thankful for the opportunity to serve others.

Introduction

A memory for a lifetime was being present at the opening service of St. Barnabas Church in Cincinnati, Ohio. I witnessed the elegance, simplicity, humility and spiritual grace of that day as human and holy spirit occupied that lovely building.

My mother often said that the preacher makes the church. For my family it was Henry McKenzie at the College Presbyterian Church in Murray, Kentucky. She would recognize that feature at St. Barnabas today. My mother also didn't let us sleep late on Sunday mornings in order for us to attend Sunday school and church which I then vigorously protested but now rejoice. My appreciation for the spiritual was elevated whether I liked it or not.

These prayers are not just evidence that I can still get up on Sunday morning for church services but were written and offered to anyone with similar spiritual needs. They were all composed during the quiet moments of the 9:30 service (and not during George's sermons).

I hope they can, in some way, be helpful to you.

ERL

Almighty God, seen and unseen;
open my eyes, my heart, and my mind
to Your light that springs forth from
You in ourselves.   Let me bask in
Your powerful quiescence allowing
the doors of my ignorance to swing
open in Your presence.   Your
supreme light shining first in
imagination, then in actualization
show that all things are possible
through faith in Your Holy Everlasting
Light of Love.
　　Amen.

Lord God Almighty, and all the heavenly hosts: hold me and help to keep me mindful of your work I try to do in Your name.   Let me awaken to your compassion through which I can protect my family from the ravages of my negative behavior by taking their pain into me.   Allow me a life long enough to know Your Truth.   In your wisdom of allowing me to assume greater burdens than I thought possible, help me be true, and always healthy for them.

　　Amen.

I reverently come before You, my Lord, my Savior, and my Creator in order that I can develop awareness and insight about the reality of the resources within me. I will always cherish Your Word that serves as my beacon, so I can learn to forgive myself as You have forgiven me and all others. I need to practice loves profound honesty with both myself and all people to know the deepest love that only You embody. With Your help, the best I have to offer can emerge for the betterment of this Your world.

Amen.

Dear Heavenly Father, we are thankful for the never-ending love You have showered upon us which appears in ways we have misunderstood because we have not known how to receive Your blessings. All that is born from our holy union of matrimony by way of word and deed is Your voice, Your will, and Your grace expressed in our blessed partner.   All our mutual expressions and movements are one and the same as Yours.   Bless us this day and for evermore.   Let us be Your appointed minister just by cherishing Your gift of the other.

Amen.

Heavenly Father, We humbly thank You for Your never ending love which You have fully bestowed to us in relationships that we sometimes misunderstand because we do not know how to receive Your blessings.

All that is born from our Holy Union of Matrimony in word and deed is in fact Your Word, Your Will, and Your Grace expressed through my cherished partner.

All intentions in behalf of the other will be evidence of Your harmonious intention.   Bless this day and every day that we are together so that our ministry with each other is possible through our appreciation of the true nature of Your gift of the other.
    Amen.

Our Heavenly Father, we pray that we can learn to speak with one another without the use of negative words or hateful references so that that the effects of our common bond Based on love will be exposed and realized with prayer and patience for guidance.   We pray that we can more fully seek the continuous light always shining in our hearts.   May we be forgiven our sins of anger and arrogance that takes your place for the sake of false protection knowing that we are truly helpless and that only your love can make us safe.   It is only Your perfect love that brings our hearts into perfect harmony.

   Amen.

Jesus Christ, my Lord and Savior, please guide me to the releasement of that which is derived from craving, of a wish for gain, and my fear of missing gain, and my fear of loss of gain, and most of all my fear of loss of imaginary gain.   Help me to know that things are never as they seem. Help me to not rely only on ruminating worry for guidance but help me to rely on the wisdom o true intuition which is your voice to me so that suffering will no longer find me.
   Amen.

Fill my heart with Your Holy Spirit of compassion so that I can always know that all things are possible during times of love as well as strife. Every moment is a blessing when I remember Your inexhaustible joy for us.   Precious Lord, just as you have endless patience with me, I need to have patience with others.   Help me to clear misconceptions about my true nature.   Help me to be enlightened to at least some of Your world which contains the presence of the deep and wonderful essence of Your love permanently endowed in all people.   I pray for this realization until I pass from this realm to Yours.
     Amen.

Today, I make this petition to my God who created me and my higher self which I call my soul whose union with my God is perfect and a reflection of infinite wisdom and compassion.
I request that love become the standard of conduct in my home.
I reverently ask for the compassion I need to forgive and to be forgiven.
I offer my complete devotion to the service of my God, who is the God throughout and request that He forgive my sins and grant my family serenity and peace forever.
  Amen.

Oh, Heavenly Father, the one protector of families, without beginning and without end, please permit me to petition thee for direction in ways that would penetrate the depths of my ignorance about love and loyalty. Please reveal to me the true extent of my selfishness. Affirm that I am born and created every day through your blessings alone which completely surround me in the form of my loved ones. I request Your help so that my family and families everywhere enjoy the true freedom of Your love.

Amen.

Dear Heavenly Father, let me appear before you as your servant for the work you have done in perfect wisdom which, daily, lets me know that Your world is just as it should be.   I humbly request that the
love in my heart will be more fully realized in my life and in the lives of those around
me.   I wish to more completely appreciate the wonderful gifts you have given me through my loving relationships, the nature of which reflects your wishes
which in turn benefits countless others. This, I pray with deep devotion, belief, and repentance.
    Amen.

Heavenly Father, who daily shows me the true spirit of life, please bestow upon me the insight and wisdom to handle generously and thoughtfully my relationship to my family and all families.   I pray, that I can open my heart to generosity and can promote the best for my mate and my offspring.   I pray, that each one of us practice the healthy life style which expresses the holiness of Your work.   I pray, that all of us find that life is exactly as we have created it for ourselves and that we can draw from Your omniscience, the knowledge that love and bliss in Your eyes is truly unconditional.   I pray, that we are all protected from fear of relationships and find that true happiness is grounded in generosity and compassion and that we can be strong enough to meet the specter of our own ignorance and isolation in order to recognize Your Light.   Your will is done when we know that You know us absolutely.   I believe that my faith in Your son Jesus Christ ushers absolute healing in all families , in Your Name.
      Amen.

Oh, Heavenly Father, source of all that I am, was, and hope to be, help me to know in deep and personal ways, the nature of my true needs so that I can want what you want and be unafraid to be my true self for all people and for all people to believe we are your children and feel grateful for all we have and also be humble for what we don't have and especially for having feelings and emotions, not discarding or hating the pain of stress or wanting only joyful feelings without attachment so we can know our true hearts as loving, accepting and compassionate. As surely as you cry with us you laugh with us. Your wisdom is truly our deliverance.

Amen.

Dear Heavenly Father, Giver of Gifts and Bestower of life.   We pray that your gift to us is the gift of new life and our gift to You is the unconditional love and cherishment of Your gift.

This child, Your child, will reflect the glory in all people.

We strive to find ourselves worthy of that task with Your patience and guidance.   As You parent us we will parent Your blessed gift throughout our lives.   In the name of Your only son Jesus Christ.

   Amen.

Oh, Heavenly Father of infinite realms and of infinite compassion, help me to know in ever deeper ways my personal and true needs so that I can want what you want for my soul and be completely unafraid as was your Son; that is to be entirely myself as He was himself.   I believe all people are your children needing to be gracious about your blessings of feelings and emotions; not discarding or hating painful feelings or accepting only pleasant ones without greed.   I also need to know acceptance and compassion.   As You surely cry with me You laugh with me.   May Your omniscient wisdom and unbound love be my deliverance.

Amen.

In the presence of the omniscience and omnipotent Lord God and the Heavenly Hosts, on my knees, I request Your comfort about the important work I wish to do.   Hasten my awakening to Your compassion through which I can comfort those who depend on me about the results of untoward behavior by more fully accepting their pain. Through Your help and their long life may they know Your Truths.   In Your infinite wisdom of allowing me to assume this virtuous task, keep me mindful and healthy for them and grateful for Your guidance expressed   every moment.

    Amen.

What name is this
I call my Lord?
What seeds are these
at first I plant?
What fields are these
I sew again?
What care is this
I give and
withhold?
What name is this
 I call my church?
What harvest is this
 I find some grain?
What form is this
 I hide from you?
What fall is this
 away from your grace?
What love is this
 I show today?
What day is this
I begin again?
What hour is this
that draws my repent after
years of quiet resent?

How do I let you raise my curtain
so that I may know You all in all?
This is the day that is every day
I will sit with You, sing with You,
laugh with
you, cry with You, and be with You in
the light
of Heaven I had mistakenly called
Hell.
    Amen.

Heavenly Father, we thank You for the never-ending love You have bestowed upon us in forms we have misunderstood because of not knowing how to receive your blessings.   All that is now born from this Holy Union of matrimony in word and deed is You word, Your will, and Your grace expressed through cherished partner of the other. Therefore, we regard all our actions and communications as if from You. On this day and for ever-more, bless our ministry with each other made possible by striving knowing the true nature of Your gifts.

   Amen.

Almighty and Everlasting God, together with Your emanation of pure love, Jesus Christ, I have arrived at this time of my life needing to be filled with faith in all that is Holy.   I realize that true faith is vast.   My faith in You must be pure.   My faith in You must be strong.   Help me purify my doubts and negative features and my yearnings to falsely understand You as a sign of my subtle doubt. Teach me that there is nothing to close or to far in Your perfect view.   You love even my doubts as well as my arrogance.   I also need to be accepting of all that I experience because all experiences are of Your world.   I must avoid extremes and thus can be filled with faith in All so that Heaven will be accessible to me as one of your children.
I know that my request will answered because Christ has destroyed death: He died for me and rose from the dead to come again in order to help me complete my sacred journey
        Amen.

Oh Heavenly Father, immaculate in patience and wisdom, please take my hand in Your wondrous hand of love and teach me the patience I sorely need because I have not fully recognized Your Holy Spirit through the tender touch of my soul mate. I vow to diligently call upon Your guidance and the blessings of this Your world to dissolve my mental confusion so that I can return the gift of Your compassion by touching her with Your love through me.

Amen.

As Jesus Christ our Lord has taught: You have not forsaken me when I think You have during moments of suffering.   Please help me not lose the knowledge that You bring forth all things great and small, pleasant and unpleasant, exhausted and filled, compassion and jealousy, as well as despair and hope.   I think there is no good or bad in Your realm.   I pray for You to surround me so that everlasting peace appears in its true form of no suffering even as we live in this world of suffering.   Teach me that death and forsakenness are without substance even when I am weak and call out to you.

   Amen.

Dear Lord, my God and my Protector: Please fill my heart with Your Holy spirit of compassion. Let me know that all things are possible during times of strife as well as times of love. Every moment is a blessing when I remember Your exquisite joy. Precious Lord, just as you have endless patience with me, may I have the enduring patience that You have shown to me. Help me to clear my misconceptions about my relationships. Lead me to the knowledge that I need to be of greater service to others. May the wondrous essence of love which is endowed by all Your children shine brightly in all of us continuously till the end of time.

Amen.

God of my fathers: Please fill my heart with your Holy Spirit of Compassion. Let me know that all things are possible during times of strife as well as times of love. Every moment is a blessing when I remember Your abundant joy. Precious Lord, just as you have had endless patience with me, may I manifest the enduring patience that You know I already possess. Help to clear my misconceptions about the true nature of relationships. Lead me to the knowledge which I need in order to be of greater service to others. May the wondrous essence of love which is endowed by all people shine brightly and continuously till the end of time through You and Your son Jesus Christ.

Amen.

This is my passionate appeal to You, my Lord and Maker from whom I yearn to feel the perfection and love of this universe.   I fervently need to feel the compassion which I know is also deep inside me.   To experience Your love more fully would be a most wonderful gift that would allow me to embrace myself with kindness and forever cease self punishing delusions.   In my mind and heart, I know, that suffering can end.   Please help me to have a kindly attitude toward myself and others knowing that with kindness I will have the favor and deference I need to be able to give what others may need from me.

   Amen.

What name is this I call my Lord?
What seeds are these at last I plant?
What fields are these I always sew?
What care is this I give and withhold?
What home is this I call my place?
What harvest is this I untimely make?
What form do I take when I hide from
You?
What fall is this away from You?
What love is this I show some days?
What way is this I repent again?
What hour is this that presses me
after days of resent?
How do I let You raise my veil?
Well now,
This is the day that is every day
I Sit with You
I Sing with You
I Stand with You
I Laugh with You
I Cry with You and
Be with You in the Light of Heaven on
earth which I had mistakenly called
Hell.
I humbly request Your forgiveness.
  Amen.

Glory to God whom I have ignored in benighted ignorance while shouting His name with joy and lifted song. I reach to Him with my soul, but alas, I do not listen.   His voice has the volume of all the combined cosmic sounds from beginningless time and I haven't heard Him because I have only listened to myself, the tiniest voice of all.   Therefore, I make request at His feet for healing, listening, and patience, knowing that He guides me at every moment of life. When I understand Him; right speech, right action, and right intent will carry me through the deepest torments and highest joys.   In this way everyone near and far shall be blessed

   Amen.

Dear Heavenly Father, immaculate in patience and wisdom, please take my hand in Your wondrous hand of love to show me the kind of patience I need because I have not fully recognized Your Holy presence through my soul mates' touch.   I vow to diligently employ Your Immaculate Blessings in this Your world.   Please dissolve my mental confusion so that I can return Your eternal compassion by touching her with Your love through me.

Amen.

As Jesus Christ our Lord has taught: You have not forsaken me when I think You have during moments of suffering.   Please help me not lose the knowledge that You bring forth all things great and small, pleasant and unpleasant, exhausted and filled, compassion and jealousy, as well as despair and hope.   I think there is no good or bad in Your realm.   I pray for You to surround me so that everlasting peace appears in its true form of no suffering even as we live in this world of suffering.   Teach me that death and forsakenness are without substance even when I am weak and call out to you.

Amen.

Epilogue

I cannot
put other gods before my Lord.
I cannot
put myself before other people.
I cannot
worship the number one.
I cannot
think that God wants to be an idol in
my devotions.
Jesus Christ said to
give up the wish for material things
that only attracts me
to the self-centered belief that God
and I are tight.
God cannot
 want to possess my adoration any
less than I want
to be possessive of adoration.
God wants me to love his special gift
of people.
Love is God.
    Amen.

Made in the USA
Columbia, SC
15 June 2020

11259488R00040